Inside a Plant

Christina Hill, M.A.

Consultants

Sally Creel, Ed.D.
Curriculum Consultant

Leann Iacuone, M.A.T., NBCT, ATC
Riverside Unified School District

Jill Tobin
California Teacher of the Year
Semi-Finalist
Burbank Unified School District

Image Credits: pp.20–21 (illustrations) Janelle Bell-Martin; all other images from Shutterstock.

Library of Congress Cataloging-in-Publication Data

Hill, Christina, author.
Inside a plant / Christina Hill; consultants, Sally Creel, Ed.D. curriculum consultant, Leann Iacuone, M.A.T., NBCT, ATC, Riverside Unified School District, Jill Tobin, California Teacher of the Year Semi-Finalist, Burbank Unified School District.
pages cm
Summary: "Plants need many things to stay alive. They need food, sun, and water. If plants have what they need, they will continue to go through a life cycle"— Provided by publisher.
Audience: K to grade 3.
Includes index.
ISBN 978-1-4807-4560-5 (pbk.)
ISBN 978-1-4807-5050-0 (ebook)
1. Plants—Juvenile literature.
2. Plant anatomy—Juvenile literature. I. Title.
QK731.H5155 2015
580—dc23

2014013143

Teacher Created Materials
5301 Oceanus Drive
Huntington Beach, CA 92649-1030
http://www.tcmpub.com

ISBN 978-1-4807-4560-5

Printed by : 465482
Printed In : Malaysia / PO#15313

Table of Contents

Plenty of Plants!

Plants grow all around us. They come in many shapes, sizes, and colors.

Crunchy carrots and leafy spinach are plants that we can eat. Big tall trees and green grass are plants, too.

Plants grow in lots of **habitats**. A cactus lives in the desert without much water. It stores water in its thick stems.

This is a desert habitat.

In rainy places, plants have waxy leaves. The wax **protects** the plants from getting too much water.

There is plenty of water in a rainforest.

Growing Up Green

A plant starts life as a seed. The seed begins to grow if it is planted in the ground. It needs water, sunlight, air, and room to grow.

Blown Away

Some seeds travel by wind before they **sprout**.

This seed has just sprouted.

The seed pushes its roots into the ground. The roots **absorb** (ab-SAWRB) water from the ground for the plant to use.

The parts of this plant work together to help it live.

Then, a stem sprouts. The stem moves the water through the plant. Finally, the plant grows leaves and sometimes flowers.

Reach for the Sky

Plant leaves grow toward sunlight. The leaves soak up sunlight to help the plant grow.

Time to Eat!

Plants need food to **survive**. That is because they are alive. But have you ever seen a plant eat?

Plants need sunlight and water to survive.

Plants are different from other living things. They make their own food inside of themselves!

A plant absorbs air, water, and sunlight. It turns them into sugar. The sugar becomes food for the plant. The food helps the plant grow and live, just like us!

This shows what a plant needs to make its food.

Tiny tubes move food and water through the plant.

Plant Families

Once a plant is grown, it releases new seeds. These seeds can sprout and start a new **life cycle** (SAHY-kuhl). Young plants look like their parent plants. That is because they grew from the same kind of seed.

A new sunflower grows from this seed.

This sunflower will release new seeds.

Around the World

Plants have **adapted** to stay alive. Some plants live on cold mountains. Other plants live in dry deserts. Some plants grow in the ocean. You can find plants almost anywhere!

These flowers have adapted to live in the cold.

Kelp is a plant that grows in the ocean.

Let's Do Science!

How does a plant get water to all of its parts? Try this and see!

What to Get

- crayons and paper
- food coloring
- plastic cup filled with water
- scissors
- white daisies

What to Do

1. Place 10 drops of food coloring into the cup of water.

2. Have an adult help you cut the stems off the daisies.

3. Place the daisies in the cup. Use crayons to draw the daisies on the paper.

4. Draw your flowers again at the end of the day. What do you notice about the petals? Why do you think this happened?

Glossary

absorb—to take in or drink

adapted—changed to be able to survive

habitats—places where plants or animals grow and live

life cycle—a series of stages that a living thing goes through as it gets older

protects—keeps safe

sprout—to begin to grow

survive—to stay alive

Index

Your Turn!

Plant Habitats

Think about where you live. What is the habitat like? Is it hot or cold? Is it dry or rainy? Make a list of the plants that grow in your area. Why do you think these plants grow well where you live?